SAVOR A TASTE
of Florida's West Coast
DUNEDIN | PALM HARBOR | TARPON SPRINGS

DUNEDIN SHORES PUBLISHING
CUSTOM BOOKS

Post Office Box 1072, Dunedin, Florida 34697

Text Copyright © 2020 by Victoria J. Bailey/All Photographs © 2020 by Victoria J. Bailey

All rights reserved. No part of this book may be reproduced or transmitted in any form or by any means, electronic or mechanical, including photocopying, recording, or by any information storage and retrieval system, without permission in writing from the publisher. For information, contact Dunedin Shores Publishing.

Library of Congress Cataloging-Publication Data on file with the Publisher.
Savor A Taste of Florida's West Coast, Signature Restaurant Recipes
Cookbook: Recipes from Dunedin, Florida, Palm Harbor, Florida, Tarpon Springs Florida.

ISBN 978-0-9980228-5-7

Publisher: VICTORIA J. BAILEY — victoria.DSP3@gmail.com
Editor: JEFF LOW — jeff@thecuckoobirdlounge.com
Graphic Design: THOMAS GRANADE — thomasgranade@gmail.com
Custom Photography: STEVEN KOVICH — kovich.com

For information about special discounts for bulk purchases,
contact Dunedin Shores Publishing at 760-219-7008
or orders@dunedinshorespublishing.com

www.dunedinshorespublishing.com

❖ FOREWORD ❖

To live on Florida's West Coast is to be awed by the beauty of nature and enjoy the wonderful vistas of land, water and sunsets, while sharing an eclectic blend of cultures. To experience the art of fine cuisine and good living, we venture out with family and friends to dine at our favorite restaurants.

Good restaurants, like good homes, have a genuine character all their own. *Savor a Taste of Florida's West Coast* celebrates that character along with the hospitality of brewers and restaurateurs. Highlighted are the culinary talents of chefs who craft perfectly-prepared meals, along with home brewers who turned professional, and wine pairings that will make for great dining memories.

While these culinary experts are understandably proud of all their creations, oftentimes one signature dish comes to represent a particular chef, and the restaurant with which they are affiliated. The purpose of this book is to share these original, straight from the heart dishes.

Savor a Taste of Florida's West Coast features one of a kind recipes — some traditional, some unexpected — that epitomize our casual and elegant Florida West Coast lifestyle. With these recipes, the chefs display their personal tastes and sense of artistry. We encourage you to visit all of the featured restaurants. You will find their contact information in the back of the book.

In recent years, craft breweries, wine cellars, and a local distillery have also become very popular — adding to your choices for a satisfying evening out on the town.

It was my pleasure getting to know the eclectic mix of chefs, owners and brewers who have greatly contributed to *Savor a Taste of Florida's West Coast*. As they will all tell you, there is no greater joy than sharing a good beer, or a glass of wine and great food, especially when it represents Florida's "Sunset Side" of Tampa Bay in Dunedin, Palm Harbor and Tarpon Springs.

Victoria Bailey

[LEFT TO RIGHT] Shardai Chaput, Café Alfresco | Jeff Sussman, H'ours Creole Smokehouse | Marguerite Allison, Marguerite's Café and Catering | Doug Clark, H'ours Creole Smokehouse
Bobbie Painter, Ozona Pig | Janson Seibert, Flanagan's Irish Pub | Karl Riedl, Bon Appétit | Sean Oliver, Flanagan's Irish Pub | Darlene Fahmey, Dunedin Coffee & Bakery Co.

[LEFT TO RIGHT] Heather & Brian Healey, Bayou Bistro and also Palm Café | Shaw Routten, Fenway Hotel and also HEW Parlor & Chophouse | Rob & Luanne Haver, Stirling Wine
Sylvia & Ismet Tzekas, Sea Sea Riders | Javier & Tina Avila, Casa Tina and also Pan y Vino

[LEFT TO RIGHT] Michael N. Bryant, Dunedin Brewery | Michael L. Bryant, Dunedin Brewery | Andrew Buckenham, Soggy Bottom Brewery | Patty Goodman, Carmelita's
Carmen Lopez, Carmelita's | Vicente Lopez, Carmelita's | Jordan Keen, Living Room | Chris Artrip, Black Pearl and also Sonder Social Club & Iron Oak New American BBQ

[LEFT TO RIGHT] Claudia Dally, Caledonia Brewing | David Dally Jr., Caledonia Brewing | Dawn Dally, Caledonia Brewing | Dave Dally III, Caledonia Brewing
Andy Polce, HOB Brewing Co. | Jon Cueni, Cueni Brewing Co. | Bren Cueni, Cueni Brewing Co. | Demetris Salivaras, Dimitri's on the Water | Andreas Salivaras, Mykonos

Bayou Bistro & Tiki
Seafood Creole.............................. 8 + 9

The Black Pearl
Duck Breast with Pumpkin Blinis........ 10 + 11

Bon Appétit Restaurant
Lobster Avocado Stack................... 12 + 13

Café Alfresco
Thai Salmon Salad...................... 14 + 15

Carmelita's Mexican Grill & Cantina
Chiles Rellenos......................... 16 + 17

Dunedin's Unique Seven Craft Breweries And One Distillery
Caledonia Brewing........................... 18
Cotherman Distilling Company............... 18
Cueni Brewing Company...................... 18
Dunedin Brewery............................ 18
HOB Brewing Company........................ 19
Soggy Bottom Brewing Company............... 19
7venth Sun Brewery......................... 19
Woodwright Brewing Company................. 19

Casa Tina
Mole Poblano............................ 20 + 21

Currents Restaurant
Crab Stuffed Whole Snapper.............. 22 + 23

Dimitri's on the Water
Crab Stuffed Shrimp with Bacon.......... 24 + 25

Dunedin Coffee Co. & Bakery
Baklava................................. 26 + 27

Fairway Grille & 19th Hole Dunedin Golf Club
Pan Seared Scallops..................... 28 + 29

Flanagan's Irish Pub
Corned Beef Tacos....................... 30 + 31

HEW Parlor & Chophouse Fenway Hotel
Filet of Beef Tartare................... 32 + 33

H'ours Creole Smokehouse
Crawfish Stuffed Flounder . . . . 34 + 35

Iron Oak New American BBQ
Pulled Pork Sandwich . . . . 36 + 37

The Living Room
Bouillabaisse . . . . 38 + 39

Marguerite's Café & Catering
Cilantro Lime Grilled Chicken . . . . 40 + 41

Marker 8 "On the Water" Tiki Bar & Grill
Spirits and Casual Fare
Pairing Guide . . . . 42 + 43

Mykonos Authentic Greek Cookery
Lamb Youvetsi . . . . 44 + 45

The Ozona Pig
Boss Hog Special . . . . 46 + 47

Palm Café Dunedin Fine Art Center
New England Lobster Roll . . . . 48 + 49

Pan y Vino
Posse's Pesto Pie . . . . 50 + 51

Sea Sea Riders Restaurant
Crusted Pecan Grouper . . . . 52 + 53

Sonder Social Club
Braised Short Ribs on Steamed Bun . . . . . . 54 + 55

Stirling Wine Premiere Wine Bar
Wine & Food Pairing Guide . . . . 56 + 57

Bayou Bistro & Tiki

Tarpon Springs

Seafood Creole

SERVES 8

3 pounds peeled deveined shrimp
2 pounds Sea scallops
3 pounds washed mussels
1 pound crawfish tails meat
Blackening seasoning
1 fresh lemon
White Rice
Scallions
¼ cup vegetable oil
½ cup white wine

Creole Sauce:
¼ cup vegetable oil
1 cup onion
1 cup green pepper
1 cup celery
3 cloves garlic
14 ounce can stewed tomatoes
1 cup tomato paste
4 cups chicken, shrimp or vegetable stock
4 teaspoons Worcestershire sauce
4 teaspoons hot sauce
2 tablespoons blackening seasoning
2 tablespoons cornstarch
1 teaspoon oregano
1 teaspoon thyme

Bayou Bistro is, "Fresh Waterfront Fare with a New England and New Orleans Flare," according to owners Heather and Brian Healey. Opening in January 2020, this is the second restaurant for these owners.

The location in Tarpon Springs is new and on the water. Heather says, "We were looking for the right opportunity and found this location that has an amazing Charter Boat Business which gives us the opportunity of buying fresh fish right off of the boats. With a great clientele of friends and family in the area, business will be booming." The new second story above the Tiki Bar will have dining and a great view of the water. Additionally, there is boat access for drinks or dinner after a fun day on the water.

Bayou Bistro's menu offers tasty, simple ingredients and fresh combinations of seafood, chicken and sausage dishes with a food style that is sure to be fresh and homemade. Brian has always had a passion for creating and cooking simple dishes which will surely make Bayou Bistro one of your favorite restaurants.

Heather and Brian are still keeping the Palm Café open at their location inside the Dunedin Fine Art Center, which has an outstanding reputation and is open for breakfast and lunch.

Method —

Heat oil in a large saucepan over medium heat. Add onion, celery, green pepper and garlic and cook until translucent. Stir in stewed tomatoes along with tomato paste and cook for 5 minutes. Add stock, Worcestershire, hot sauce and blackening seasoning and bring to a boil. Mix cornstarch with cold water and add to boiling sauce to thicken. Take off heat and add herbs and green onions. Set aside.

Heat quarter cup of vegetable oil in large saucepan and sear scallops, flipping scallops once. Add shrimp and cook until almost done. Add mussels and cook until shells open. Add crawfish tails and wine and reduce. Add creole sauce just to heat (do not cook).

Plating: Serve Seafood Creole over the rice. Garnish with chopped scallions on top. Serve with French bread.

Wine and Spirit Pairing —

Beer of your choice

Heather Healey

Chef Brian Healey

The Black Pearl

Dunedin on Main

Duck Breast with Pumpkin Blinis

SERVES 6

6 trimmed duck breast
½ cup kosher salt
2 teaspoons smoked paprika
¼ cup dark brown sugar

Blinis Pancakes:
1 small pumpkin (1-2 pounds)
2 cups all-purpose flour
3 whole eggs
1 large size egg yolk
1½ teaspoon kosher salt
½ teaspoon ground black cardamom
½ teaspoon ground nutmeg
1 teaspoon ground dry ginger
2 tablespoons brown sugar
¼ teaspoon turmeric (optional for color)
2 tablespoons butter
3 cups half and half

Pomegranate Gastrique Sauce:
8 ounces pomegranate juice
6 ounces red wine vinegar
½ cup sugar
2 ounces Tawney Port

Plating:
6 tablespoons toasted candied pecans
6 tablespoons orange marmalade
Citrus zest
Maple syrup
Pomegranate seeds

The Black Pearl has been an institution in Pinellas County for over two decades. Acquired by the Feinstein Group in 2014, The Black Pearl is one of their premier properties. Chef Christopher Artrip, voted, "Best Chef Tampa Bay," leads their amazing culinary team in creating new and delicious recipes. The Black Pearl serves French-New American Cuisine and is the number one spot for a special occasion or date night out.

Chef Chris says, " Life is too short to eat bad food. I chose this recipe as my signature dish because after creating a rendition of it for a wine dinner, I got multiple requests and added it to our menu."

Method —

Duck Breast: Rub the meat side of duck breast with ingredients. Place duck in a pre-heated pan duck skin side down with a touch of oil in the pan. Cook for about 7 minutes until skin is crispy. Flip duck over on the meat side, and set pan aside. This will bring duck breast to a medium (pinkish) temperature.

Pumpkin Blinis: Cut pumpkin in half and place face down on a greased baking pan in a 400°F oven. Cook for 75 minutes, and cool for 30 minutes so it doesn't cook your eggs. Scoop out the seeds, wash the pulp off, ready to roast for snacking later. Blend pumpkin and ingredients together in a blender and transfer to a squeeze bottle. Place butter in a Teflon pan. Squeeze mini dabs of pumpkin batter into the pan about 2-3 inches apart. Cook for 1 minute on one side, then flip pancakes and cook for 45 seconds, until you see the edges form on the pancakes. Remove and place pancakes on paper towels.

Pomegranate Gastrique: Place all ingredients in a medium size saucepan and heat to Medium High. Reduce the volume of the sauce by 3/4 until syrupy (usually 20-30 minutes). Keep an eye on it as stove temperatures can vary. Once it starts bubbling with tiny surface bubbles then it's done. Transfer to a squeeze bottle or another container for serving later.

Plating: Place pancakes on plate then add sliced duck breast on top. Drizzle the pomegranate and place small dots on the plate. Sprinkle pomegranate seeds or other toppings sporadically. Quail eggs optional.

Wine and Spirit Pairing —

Russian River Valley Emeritus Pino Noir

Chef Christopher Artrip   Zachery Feinstein

Bon Appétit Restaurant

Dunedin Waterfront

Lobster Avocado Stack

SERVES 2

2 lobsters
2 ripe avocados, seeded, skinned, and diced
1 tablespoon fresh-squeezed lime juice
1 tablespoon sweet diced onions
¼ teaspoon salt
2 tablespoons fresh cilantro leaf
1 tablespoon diced celery

On the shores of St. Joseph Sound sits Dunedin's most established restaurant, Bon Appétit, owned by Peter Kreuziger and Chef Karl Riedl. Since opening its doors in 1976, the restaurant has become quite an area landmark, offering award-winning entrées and exceptional service, and earning titles like, *'America's Most Scenic Restaurant'* for its incredible waterfront views.

Bon Appétit offers an eclectic blend of European and American-style cuisine, their chefs using simple, fresh ingredients, changing the menu seasonally. Choices of delicious seafood, signature gourmet dishes and everyday favorites provide an exciting variety. The Lobster Avocado Stack, a popular choice, is a perfect example. "Chilled lobster and avocado complement each other perfectly when blended with just the right seasoning," says Executive Chef Karl Riedl.

In addition to the mouthwatering menu, Bon Appétit offers an extensive wine selection, full bar service and an elegant, comfortable atmosphere. Enjoy breathtaking waterfront views and stunning sunsets while dining indoors or out on the terrace or at the outdoor bar. For a lunch break or to celebrate a special occasion, it doesn't get any better than Bon Appétit!

Method —

Mix all ingredients in a small bowl. When the lobsters are cold remove the tail and claw. Carefully shell them, discarding the cartilage. Cut the tail into quarter-inch thick medallions. Dice the knuckle meat. Cut the claw meat in half to save for the garnish. Mix the tail and knuckle meat with two tablespoons of Hellman's mayonnaise, celery, salt, white pepper and a squeeze of fresh lemon.

Plate: To stack, use a 3 to 4 inch pastry ring, starting with the avocado mixture at the bottom. Add the lobster mixture and garnish with claws and add cilantro to taste.

Wine and Spirit Pairing —

White Oak Sauvignon Blanc

Peter W. Kreuziger, Proprietor

Chef Karl Heinz Riedl, Proprietor

Café Alfresco

Dunedin on Main

Thai Salmon Salad

SERVES 4

Salmon:
4 salmon filets
   (6 ounces each)
½ cup sesame seeds (black & white)

Salad:
8 cups fresh spinach
2 cups shredded cabbage (purple & green)
4 beef steak tomatoes (diced)
½ cup matchstick carrots

Crispy Wonton Strips:
2 cups oil
2 egg roll wrappers

Dressing:
2 cups vegetable oil
3 tablespoons soy sauce
3 tablespoons honey
¼ cup mandarin orange segments
¼ cup orange marmalade
½ teaspoon granulated garlic
4 tablespoons sesame oil
½ cup rice wine vinegar
6 fresh basil leaves

A neighborhood favorite since 1995, Café Alfresco is known for its friendly service, reasonable prices and delicious food. Warm smiles greet each guest, followed by professional, gracious service. "Café Alfresco is where the locals and visitors like to eat," says co-owner Peter Kreuziger. "We're on a first name basis with many of our guests."

A delightful feature is the restaurant's oversized windows allowing guests to view all the action while they dine. When Florida's weather is at its best, the outdoor patio is the perfect spot to enjoy a glass of wine, a craft beer or a signature cocktail while overlooking the Pinellas Trail.

The menu features a wonderful mix of American style favorites along with hints of international inspiration. Delicious sandwiches, exciting salads, pasta dishes and hearty home-style meals are found in addition to the chef's daily lunch and dinner specials. Don't forget dessert! Café Alfresco's dessert case is filled with favorites like Florida Key Lime Pie and, "The best" Blueberry Pie — homemade of course.

Café Alfresco is owned by Peter Kreuziger and Karl Riedl of the Bon Appétit Group.

Method —

Salmon: Place one side of Salmon Filet on the blended sesame seeds. Heat non-stick sauté pan with enough oil to coat the bottom of the pan. Sear Salmon sesame seed side down, flip once so the filet is golden brown. Continue to cook Salmon in oven 350°F until it reaches 145°F (approximately 5 to 8 minutes).

Salad: Place 2 cups fresh Spinach in your desired bowl along with ½ cup cabbage. Garnish with diced beefsteak tomatoes, matchstick carrots and crispy wonton strips.

Dressing: Rough-chop mandarin orange segments set aside, then place all ingredients (except mandarin orange segments) in blender, cover and blend on medium speed for 1 minute. Transfer to a bowl, mix the chopped mandarin orange segments into blended dressing and refrigerate.

Crispy Wonton Strips: Thaw egg roll wrappers, once at pliable temperature. Cut into ½ inch strips. In a small pot, heat oil and fry egg roll wrappers until golden brown. Remove from oil, drain well (use paper towel to absorb excess oil). Place over salad.

Wine and Spirit Pairing —

New Zealand Frenzy Sauvignon Blanc

Peter W. Kreuziger, Proprietor

Chef Karl Heinz Riedl, Proprietor

Carmelita's

Mexican Grill and Cantina

Chiles Rellenos

SERVES 6

6 fresh poblano peppers
   (or mild whole green chiles)
6 eggs
½ pound Oaxaca or
   Monterrey Jack Cheese
¼ cup of flour
2 cups corn oil
1 tablespoon flour
Salt or Mexican seasoning

Carmelita's Mexican Restaurant was first established in 1983 in St. Petersburg, Florida with only 50 seats. Vicente and Carmelita Lopez moved to St. Petersburg, Florida from Michigan in 1973 and found no Mexican restaurants in the area. After 10 years of serving their friends and family home-cooked traditional meals, Vicente felt there was definitely a need for a Mexican restaurant in St. Petersburg.

Carmelita recalls many fond memories growing up with family in Texas and Michigan. She and her mother, Katy, would always cook the family meals. "So when it came time to putting a restaurant menu together," Carmelita says, "my mom and I just kept cooking the sauces and tweaking dishes until they tasted 'just right.'"

With the help of many family members and countless loyal employees, Carmelita and Vicente continue to bring great traditional Mexican dishes to the tables of discerning patrons. In 2014, they opened Carmelita's Mexican Grill and Cantina in Dunedin, offering that same friendly traditional feel with a high level of devoted service. Of course, they still use the recipes that made Carmelita's one of the most beloved Mexican restaurants, now with five locations in Pinellas County. A customer favorite is their Chiles Rellenos. Customers are always asking Vicente if there is a real Carmelita and he answers, "Yes, I married her!"

Method —

Heat one cup of oil and poblano chilies in the oil for a few minutes until they are lightly charred on both sides. Place on the tray and cover with a paper towel. After a few minutes check the chilies. Once the skin comes off easily peel each chile. Cut a slit almost the full length of each chile, remove the seeds and leave the stem attached. Stuff each chile with cheese. Place on a tray and cover them with plastic wrap then place in the refrigerator for a few hours.

Whip the egg whites on a high speed with an electric mixer until stiff peaks form. Heat the other cup of oil. Beat the egg yolks with one tablespoon of flour and salt. Mix yolk into egg whites and stir until you have a thick paste.

Roll each chile in the flour and dip it into the egg batter. Coating each chile evenly, place in some oil and fry seam side down on medium heat for a few seconds until each side is golden brown. Place on paper towel to drain.

Wine and Spirit Pairing —

Draft Dos Equis Amber Beer

Vicente Lopez

Carmen Lopez

Dunedin's Unique 7

CALEDONIA BREWING opened in April 2017 in the historic 1925 Dunedin Times building on Main Street. Started by friends, family and beer enthusiasts who were home brewers, they decided to take their passion and skills to the next level. Known for their Rat Arsed Scotch Ale and a wide selection of IPAs, Caledonia celebrates Dunedin's Scottish heritage which is featured in their logo and décor.

COTHERMAN DISTILLING COMPANY is the premiere family-owned business opened in 2014, and remains the only distillery in Dunedin. They currently distill over 20 unique spirits in house and work in symbiosis with the Seven local brewers regarding ingredients, manufacturing, cellaring and promotion. The American Single Malt Whiskey is made from malted barley spirit aged in new charred American oak barrels. The best and costliest ingredients are used for both bourbon and Scotch. Other products include 727 Vodka, Half-Mine Gin, and Palmer's Tropical line of Rums including silver, gold, dark, spiced and distiller's reserve.

CUENI BREWING COMPANY was a dream fired up on the kitchen stove of Jon Cueni. Like many other professionals he started as a home brewer. Opened in late 2016 with their unique take on Belgian and English Ales, Cueni is known for its friendly staff and outstanding beer. They have won many awards, most recently Gold at the 2019 US Beer Open for their Curious Gourd Pumpkin Ale.

DUNEDIN BREWERY is the oldest microbrewery in Florida, owned and operated by Michael and Kandi Bryant. They started fermenting in 1996. In addition to standard beers like Apricot Peach Ale and Flashlight Lager, they are also proud to make available many seasonal and specialty upscale brews. The tasting room is known for its on-site kitchen and offers some of the best live music in the entire Tampa Bay Area.

Craft Breweries
1 Distillery

HOB BREWING COMPANY was opened in February 2009 by Andy Polce and Rick Clemo, quickly becoming one of America's Top 100 Beer Bars. With over a decade of experience bringing craft beer to the masses, the HOB Beers were designed and created with maximum likability and appeal, winning three Best Beer Medals in 2019. Enjoy also their new trail side patio.

SOGGY BOTTOM BREWING COMPANY was started by three local bartenders. Andrew Buckenham, Cary Lamb and Lucas Rizor began their home brewing in 2009 just for fun and it quickly became their passion. Soggy Bottom opened in April 2017 and is known for having rotating styles, the result of their being creative and thinking "Out of the Barrel." The brewery has an old and rustic vibe, a great staff and has been well received by locals and visitors.

7VENTH SUN BREWERY opens every day at noon, and proudly offers a friendly atmosphere in which to enjoy their unique IPAs, Sours, Stouts and Oak/Barrel-Aged Beers that are a perfect match for Florida lifestyles. Featured are sour beers on tap every week and to-go options such as growlers, bottles and six-pack cans.

WOODWRIGHT BREWING COMPANY was created by Eunice and Grant Painter with help from friends but actually began as a mere hobby on Eunice's kitchen stove. It is now a World Class brewing system all the while hidden away in the back corner of the historic Dunedin Woodwright building, home of the family's heirloom woodworking business. Eunice had a longtime interest in German brews and after several years honing her craft, she now features 18 beers on tap including a Hefeweizen, German Alt, and Kolsch. Eventually, the brewery, tasting room, beer garden and concert venues eclipsed the woodworking business. In 2019, Eunice's Oktoberfest Marzen was named, "Best Small Batch Beer" in Florida.

Casa Tina

Fresh Healthy Authentic Mexican

Mole Poblano

SERVES 6-8

Mole Sauce:
½ pound chile pasilla
½ pound chile ancho
1 box raisins
1 large onion
½ cup garlic
1½ cups almonds
1 cup sesame seeds
1 tablespoon black pepper
1 tablespoon white pepper
1 tablespoon cumin
3 tablespoons cinnamon
3 boxes chocolate abuelita

Enchiladas:
6-8 corn tortillas
2 cups Queso Fresco shredded cheese
1 cup Mozzarella cheese shredded
3 cups shredded chicken
Vegan Options

Javier and Tina Avila met at his restaurant, Señor Frog's located in Miami's Coconut Grove. He was running the restaurant and she was looking for a job. Javier is originally from Mazatlán, Mexico where he began his career. Tina was raised in Philadelphia, Pennsylvania.

After honing their culinary skills in Miami, Javier and Tina moved to Dunedin.

Tina says, "28 years after stumbling upon the quaint town of Dunedin we opened Casa Tina's. We were looking for a slower-paced, family-friendly community and thought Dunedin would be the perfect place to showcase our love of Mexican cuisine while raising our children." Between Javier's Mexican heritage and Tina's desire for healthy food, they knew they had the perfect mix for the outdoor Florida lifestyle. Casa Tina's authentic recipes feature tropical ingredients mixed with traditional Mexican herbs and spices.

"Everyone has a Mexican grandma with her own unique special Mole sauce. Our Mole Poblano dish has all the indigenous ingredients, including chocolate, chilies and nuts — all blended to create a warm and exotic sauce unlike any other. We have been cooking this recipe for 35 years. Casa Tina's Mole Poblano has been on the menu from the beginning and is one our best examples of Mexican cuisine with all of its complexity."

Method —

Boil pasilla and ancho chiles for 15 minutes. In a sauté pan cook chopped garlic and onions, adding sesame, almonds, pepper, cinnamon and cumin. Drain peppers and conserve some of the chile water. Place chiles in blender, add raisins and blend with some chile water as needed until liquefied.

Pour sautéed items and blended liquid into a large stock pot and add chocolate. Cook the entire mixture for 30 minutes stirring frequently.

Place a large ladle of sauce in a frying pan over medium heat. Moisten soft corn tortillas in sauce and add shredded chicken and Mozzarella and Queso Fresco cheese. For a vegan option, add your favorite vegetable instead of chicken. Fold tortilla over and allow to heat for approximately for 1 minute. Remove from pan and serve on a platter with sprinkled sesame seeds and cilantro.

Serving Suggestion: Shredded Chicken or Vegetarian Enchiladas (as seen in photo).

Wine and Spirit Pairing —

Grayson Cabernet

Tina Marie Avila

Chef Javier Avila

Currents Restaurant

Tarpon Springs

Crab Stuffed Whole Snapper

SERVES 1

Sweet Chili Sauce:
1 tablespoon garlic
10 dried chili peppers
1 teaspoon salt
¼ cup water
¼ cup rice wine vinegar
2 tablespoons cornstarch slurry

Fish:
1-1½ pound whole Red Snapper
1 cup rice flour
1 tablespoon salt
1 tablespoon garlic powder
1 tablespoon onion powder
1 tablespoon white pepper
½ cup cornstarch

Crab Cake:
1 ounce jumbo lump crab meat
1 ounce claw meat
1 tablespoon mayonnaise
1 tablespoon grain mustard
1 teaspoon Worcestershire
½ cup lemon juice
1 teaspoon Old Bay seasoning
1 stalk celery
½ onion
1 teaspoon garlic
1 egg

The port city of Tarpon Springs was founded by Greek sponge divers and is known for its authentic Grecian food. It is rewarding, therefore, to find a contemporary restaurant with such elegance and charm, located in the center of town on Tarpon Avenue, which is lined with antique and art shops. This is where a young, but experienced Tracey Swade designed Current's to accent this artistic setting and offer a sophisticated cuisine, thus providing a unique dining experience for her guests. Tracey transformed the interior of this brick building constructed in 1905, an historic location. Featured are paintings on muted faux walls, rich brocade booths, and a long glorious wooden bar.

Opened in 2009, this intimate boutique restaurant is inspired by fresh concepts of culinary art and has joined the gluten-free movement. Featuring gourmet dining right in the heart of downtown Tarpon Springs, Currents Restaurant also serves great burgers, steaks and fresh seafood plus specialty martini cocktails, unique wines and tapas pairings monthly.

The new, "Third Space Event Hall" originally served as the Tarpon Springs Motion Theatre from 1909 to 1919, with high ceilings and an entire wall of vintage brick and original wood floors. It is now available for any business, social or special occasion event.

Method —

Sweet Chili Sauce: In a small pan add all ingredients to make the Sweet Chili Sauce, except for the cornstarch. Bring ingredients to a slow boil until you reduce by half. While still boiling, add the cornstarch slurry whisking or stirring constantly until it is well-incorporated and the sauce starts to thicken. Set aside.

Cornstarch Slurry: Mix 1 tablespoon cornstarch with 1 to 2 tablespoons of water to make a liquid-like paste.

Red Snapper. Score the whole fish. Mix your rice flour, salt, garlic powder, onion powder and white pepper together. Toss the Snapper in the bowl covering with mixture. Deep fry Snapper for about eight minutes. In a mixing bowl combine all ingredients except the crab. Slowly fold crab into the ingredients and allow to rest for 10 minutes. In a butter saucepan sauté crab until golden brown.

Plating: Serve fish topped with crab mixture...or spooned over the top.

Wine and Spirit Pairing —

Sonoma Cutrer Chardonnay

Tracey Swade

Chef Joseph Rivera

Dimitri's on the Water

Tarpon Springs

Crab Stuffed Shrimp with Bacon

SERVES 2

8 large deveined shrimp
8 slices apple wood bacon
3 ounces Blackening seasoning

Sauce Reduction:
2 cups balsamic vinegar
1 cup teriyaki sauce
½ cup pineapple juice
½ cup apple juice
1 whole orange
1 lemongrass stalk
2 small shallots
1 habanero pepper
¼ cup crumbled Feta cheese
3 ounces extra virgin olive oil
3 tablespoons minced garlic
Salt and pepper to taste

Crab Mixture:
12 ounces jumbo lump crabmeat
3 ounces mayonnaise
Juice of one ½ lemon
1 celery stalk
1 teaspoon Worcestershire
6 tablespoons chopped parsley
Salt and pepper to taste

Dimitri's on the Water is located in Tarpon Springs, known for its Greek Heritage and as the *Sponge Capital of the World.* Demetrios Salivaras' parents are originally from the Greek Island of Kimilos and came to Tarpon Springs to open a restaurant called Mykonos, which is across the street from Dimitri's. Dimitri says, "Growing up in my father's business, meant that this business chose me."

Opened in 2010, Dimitri's on the Water is located right on the Gulf of Mexico. Enjoy dining outside where there is a full service bar on the patio.

"The style of our menu is New Fusion Greek Cuisine. The key is using all the local fresh seafood options right from the boat, to the dock, to the kitchen. We strive to give the best service with high quality seafood and fresh domestic produce."

Dimitri's signature dish is one of their customers' favorites. They use a special technique in the preparation which is to par-cook the bacon before wrapping the shrimp, so that the bacon stays crispy. They also use an imported Feta cheese in the reduction because the creamier the cheese, the better.

Dimitri says, "My father Andreas always told me to have discipline and commitment and I would be successful."

Method —

Mince shallots, garlic and habanero pepper. Snap lemongrass in half and brown in the olive oil. Add all other ingredients and begin to reduce. Cut orange into fours and add to the sauce reduction. Pour in some water (if needed) in order to get the consistency you want for the sauce reduction. Reduce to a consistency of a syrup. Let sauce cool until you are able to add the Feta cheese so that it will not melt away.

Mix all crab ingredients together. Keep crab in chunks while mixing.

While sauce reduces, butterfly the shrimp. Stuff shrimp with crab meat and dredge in Blackening seasoning. Wrap stuffed shrimp with bacon and bake at 400°F until golden brown.

Plating: Spoon sauce on plate, then add the crab-stuffed shrimp wrapped in bacon. Garnish with scallions.

Wine and Spirit Pairing —

Louis Martini Cabernet Sauvignon

Demetrios A. Salivaras

Dunedin Coffee Co. & Bakery

Dunedin

 Baklava

SERVES 24

Filling
4 cups ground walnuts
8 tablespoons sugar
1 tablespoon cinnamon
1 box phyllo pastry dough sheets (thaw if frozen)
2 sticks salted butter (melted)
4 tablespoons shortening (melted)

Syrup
1½ cups sugar
1 cup water
Juice of one ½ lime
1 teaspoon vanilla

Great coffee with homemade pastries and quiche, along with more of the small-town atmosphere that Dunedin is known for, makes Dunedin Coffee Company & Bakery a truly great place for locals and visitors to come and meet.

Owners Darlene and Wagdy use the best quality ingredients to make all of their tasty treats. Their cuisine is not unlike what you would find in an upscale European Market. In fact, many visitors around the world enjoy Dunedin Coffee Company & Bakery because it reminds them of their home.

"Our signature dish is 'Baklava' which we have perfected over time. It's homemade and doesn't use any honey in the syrup. It's from the Egyptian culture which is our birthplace, and goes great with the quality coffees that are specially blended, roasted and ground daily."

Method —

Filling Mixture: Mix walnuts, sugar and cinnamon together in a bowl and set aside.

Butter Mixture: Melt butter and shortening together.

Open box of phyllo dough and divide into three sections. Start with melted butter and shortening in bottom of 9" x 11" square cake pan. Take one-third of the dough and start layering it in the pan, putting some of melted butter mixture between layers.

Once one-third of dough is in the pan, take half of the filling mixture and spread over dough. Place one sheet over the filling then pour butter mixture, coating it well. Place one sheet over this slowly as to not move it.

Continue layering two-thirds of dough while putting some of the melted butter mixture in between layers. When you're done with the two-thirds of dough, repeat the same process as you did with the one-third dough and nut mixture, using one phyllo dough sheet with butter mixture. Continue on with third section of dough using same process. When you get to the top layer, cut dough into desired shape and pour remaining butter mixture over the top.

Preheat your oven to 350°F and bake for 30 minutes until the top is golden.

Syrup: Boil sugar and water together slowly. Add squeezed lime and vanilla. Let mixture boil slowly until syrup thickens. Pour over the pastry after it's done baking.

Darlene Fahmey

Fairway Grille & 19th Hole

Dunedin Golf Club

Pan Seared Scallops

SERVES 2

1-1¼ pounds scallops
2 teaspoons unsalted butter
2 teaspoons olive oil
Kosher salt & black pepper to taste

Bacon Jam:
1½ pounds bacon
¾ cup espresso
½ cup apple cider vinegar
½ cup brown sugar
¼ cup maple syrup

Sweet Potato Au Gratin:
2 large uncooked potatoes, peeled and sliced ¼" thick
2 cups heavy whipping cream
¾ teaspoon salt
⅛ teaspoon ground nutmeg
3 tablespoons Parmesan cheese
Pinch of black pepper

The Dunedin Golf Club, originally Dunedin Country Club, is rich with its history and tradition. The Club is open to the public and offers affordable memberships. The course, designed by the world renowned golf course architect Donald Ross, opened January 1, 1927. Dunedin Golf Club, from 1945 through 1962 was the original home of the PGA of America, hosting 18 Senior Tour Championships. Dunedin Golf Club is one of the top clubs in the area and has won four years in a row the, "Reader's Choice" award for Best Golf Club by the *Tampa Bay Newspaper*.

Dunedin Golf Club's chef and management agree they provide the best of all worlds. Try their awesome burgers and beer or fine dining, paired with a bottle of wine. "We change our menu seasonally to give you the freshest ingredients. Come in and join us for lunch, dinner or that special event. Our best advertisement is word of mouth generated by happy customers," says General Manager, Ken Nyhus CCM, CCE.

Method —

Bacon Jam: In a large skillet over medium heat, cook bacon until fat is rendered and bacon is lightly brown, about 20 minutes. Place bacon on paper towels to drain. In the same skillet add the espresso, vinegar, brown sugar and maple syrup and bring to boil. In the same skillet stir and scrape up any browned bits for 2 minutes and add the bacon to the skillet and combine. Let the bacon cool slightly before transferring to a food processor, then pulse until coarsely chopped. Spoon bacon jam into a resealable container and refrigerate up to four weeks.

Sweet Potato Au Gratin: In 8" square greased baking dish, line the bottom with potatoes, sprinkle with Parmesan cheese alternating layers. Add cream, salt, nutmeg and pepper in a bowl, mixing well and pour over the potatoes. Sprinkle Parmesan over the top layer of the potatoes. Oven bake uncovered at 375°F until potatoes are tender, about 40 to 45 minutes.

Scallops: Remove small side muscle from the scallops, rinse with cold water and thoroughly pat dry. Add butter and oil to 12" or 14" saucepan on high heat. Salt and pepper the scallops. Once the butter and oil begin to smoke gently add the scallops and sear for 1½ minutes on each side.

Plating: Use a ring mold (can find at a restaurant supply or online) and press into the sweet potato au gratin about six times, removing any excess to a side plate. You will have round molds of sweet potatoes. Using a spatula take potatoes placing them on the plates in a row. Top sweet potatoes with your golden-brown scallops. Spoon your bacon jam over the scallops.

Chef Adrienne Morris

Ken Nyhus

Flanagan's Irish Pub

Dunedin on Main

Corned Beef Tacos

SERVES 10

4-5 pounds corned beef brisket
1 pint Guinness beer
1 pint cold water

Horseradish Dressing:
1 cup mayonnaise
⅓ cup sour cream
2 ounces whole grain mustard
1 teaspoon granulated garlic
1 teaspoon granulated onion
1 teaspoon cracked black pepper
½ teaspoon salt
2 ounces horseradish (drained)

Coleslaw:
Half of a head green cabbage (shredded)
1 carrot peel and shredded

Other Ingredients:
Corn tortillas
Shredded cheddar cheese
Crispy bacon
Jalapeños
Green scallions
Parsley

The original Flanagan's Hunt Irish Pub was opened in 1992 by Alex Pringle and Michelle Glen, located on the east end of Main Street in an already thriving downtown Dunedin. After years of success Michelle sold her share of the pub to Noel and Trina Cooney who ran the pub with their son, Dale.

In August of 2016, a new owner came on the scene when Jason Seibert bought the pub. The previous owners had created the most successful St. Patrick's Day celebration in the county and Jason continues that legacy: "We have grown the event which today draws about 50,000 attendees with lots of good food, some brews, some whiskey and different bands from morning 'til late hours in the evening. Flanagan's current focus is on great Irish food with chef Sean Oliver at the helm of the kitchen."

Jason is now personally inviting you and yours to share a pint or two and become members of their vast and ever-growing Flanagan's Family. They are open seven days a week — on the weekends featuring authentic Irish rebel music. "Come and join us."

Method —

Cook corned beef brisket in a roasting pan with fat side up. Add one pint of Guinness beer and one pint of cold water. Cover pan tightly with foil and cook in oven at 200°F for 12 hours. Remove from the oven and carefully remove foil. Drain liquid and fat from the meat. Cut against the grain into about one inch strips, shredding meat with a fork.

Coleslaw: Mix all ingredients of the dressing in a bowl. In a larger bowl toss shredded cabbage and peeled carrots. Mix dressing with cabbage and carrot slaw.

Tacos: Heat corn tortillas in a skillet or on the grill. Melt one ounce shredded cheese on each corn tortilla. Add two ounces of shredded corned beef to each taco and two ounces horseradish slaw. Finally, dress taco with crispy bacon, sliced green scallions, fresh jalapeños and a pinch of chopped parsley.

Wine and Spirit Pairing —

Enjoy with a pint of Guinness.

Jason Seibert   Chef Sean Oliver

HEW Parlor & Chophouse

Fenway Hotel

Filet of Beef Tartare

SERVES 1

Steak Tartare:
3½ ounces hand-minced raw filet mignon
2½ tablespoons tartare dressing
2 ounces creamy horseradish tarragon sauce
Salt and pepper to taste
1 teaspoon pickled mustard seed
2 charred baby pearl onions, broken up into petals
1 egg yolk
Tiny edible flowers
Maldon sea salt
Ciabatta bread, grilled with olive oil & salt
Onion ash

Tartare Dressing:
4 ounces olive oil
2 ounces red wine vinegar
3 ounces Worcestershire sauce
1 ounce chopped basil
½ ounce chopped raw shallots
½ ounce chopped raw garlic
1 teaspoon Dijon mustard

Built in 1924, Fenway Hotel is an icon of the jazz age. This Grand Lady of Dunedin re-opened its doors in 2018, heralding the destination's first boutique luxury hotel, steeped in a musical heritage and wrapped in stunning Mediterranean revival architecture.

As its signature dining outlet, HEW Parlor & Chophouse drew its name from the original architect of the Fenway, Herman Everett Wendell. To 'hew' also means to cut or chop.

Comprised of three show-stopping elements, each section can be identified by a slightly different rhythm. Discover the intimate parlor bar, showcasing an extensive whiskey and Scotch collection inspired by Dunedin's Scottish heritage, and accentuated by water views. The chef's dining bar affords front seat views of the hustle and bustle of their production kitchen.

Chophouse cuts and chef-driven seasonal preparations are the specialty, harmonized effortlessly by creatively constructed vegetarian options.

Method —

Tartare Dressing: In a blender, blend everything except oil. Emulsify oil over medium speed.

Plating: In a mixing bowl place diced steak, dress with tartare dressing and season with salt and pepper. On a plate, spoon or brush creamy horseradish tarragon. Place dressed tartare on top of creamy horseradish tarragon. On top of steak tartare, place an indentation and spoon egg yolk on top then season with maldon. Place pickled mustard seeds and charred onions on top of meat.

Garnish: Place tiny edible flowers along with onion ash and grilled ciabatta crostini.

Wine and Spirit Pairing —

Pairs well with a California Cabernet.

Shawn Routten

H'ours Creole Smokehouse

Tarpon Springs

Crawfish Stuffed Flounder

SERVES 6

6 six-ounce Flounders

Crawfish and Shrimp Stuffing:
1 Spanish onion chopped
¼ stalk celery
4 ounces fresh basil chopped
1 pound shrimp
2 whole roasted reds peppers
    (fresh or in a jar)
2 tablespoons garlic
1 pound butter
Blackened and creole seasoning to taste
Salt, pepper, and Tabasco to taste
2 pounds of Crawfish or Crab Meat
4 tablespoons lemon juice
    (2 lemons)
3 ounces mayonnaise
3 eggs
2 ounces Dijon mustard
1 cup breadcrumbs

Sauce:
1 cup Sauvignon Blanc wine
1 cup heavy cream
¼ cup capers
2 ounces shallots chopped
4 tablespoons lemon juice
    (2 lemons)
2 tablespoons dill
3 cups chicken stock
Butter chunks

New to Tarpon Springs in October 2019, H'ours Creole Smokehouse is a collaboration of three partners who took a 1905 Historic Victorian, completely renovated and transformed it from an old house to a new restaurant, then began to serve fine New Orleans fare sourcing Florida seafood. The partners chose Tarpon Springs because they wanted to be part of its surging popularity.

The flavor influence comes from Doug Clark's mom, Barb, a chef who forced him to move to New Orleans and learn how to cook, where he fell in love with the cuisine. H'ours is a unique creation that is reminiscent of marathon sessions between Doug Clark and Jeff Sussman at the kitchen table trying to craft their idea for a World Class dining destination.

H'ours is a scratch kitchen so their menu changes daily based on local seafood availability, and of course it is all about the service because as Chef Jeff Sussman says, "We want our guests to feel at home, so we cook nothing but great food with fresh ingredients. Stuffed Flounder is our signature dish and we use Florida shrimp and New Orleans crawfish for the stuffing."

Method —

Stuffing: Heat oil, then add butter, onion, peppers, garlic, celery, basil, shrimp and crawfish. Add blackened seasonings to taste. Strain the mixture and set aside to cool. If using a pre-packaged crawfish, strain before putting in blender. Gradually add crawfish mixture and stuffing mixture in blender. Pulse in blender keeping it somewhat chunky. Refrigerate 5 to 10 minutes until mixture is cold. Pour ingredients from blender into a mixing bowl. Add eggs, mustard, mayo, Tabasco and breadcrumbs then mix well. Refrigerate for 5 to 10 minutes. If mixture is wet, fold in more breadcrumbs. Divide stuffing in two to three ounce portions.

Fish: Season fish with creole spices on both sides. Take two to three ounces of stuffing at the small end of the fish and roll up like a pinwheel. Pour oil in pan and sear fish on both sides on high heat. Add wine, chicken stock and the juice of two lemons. Finish by cooking in 400°F oven for about 8 minutes.

Sauce: In the same saucepan add wine and cream. Bring to a boil. Reduce sauce and add dill, capers and lemon. When thickened, turn off heat. Add cold chunks of butter until it thickens. Strain sauce.

Plating: Lay grilled asparagus in center of plate. Add rice on top of asparagus. Add fish on of top of rice. Ladle sauce on edge of fish and garnish with lemon wheel, fresh dill, capers and tomatoes.

Wine and Spirit Pairing —

Escape IPA or Garden District Martini – made with lemon ginger

Chef Jeff Sussman, Owner

Chef Doug Clark, Owner

Iron Oak New American BBQ

Palm Harbor

Pulled Pork Sandwich

SERVES 6-8

6 nine-pound pork butt
 (Duroc preferred)
Salted Pretzel Brioche

Pork Rub:
½ cup dark brown sugar
2 tablespoons smoked hot paprika
3 tablespoons Hungarian sweet paprika
½ kosher salt
1 tablespoon dark chili powder
1 tablespoon Coleman dry mustard
2 tablespoons ground black pepper
1 teaspoon Rosal Hanout powder

The Iron Oak New American BBQ opened in May 2018, downtown in historic Palm Harbor. Chef Christopher Artrip says, "I went to Middle School in the Palm Harbor area which helped influence me with choosing this type of cuisine. The meats are all of the highest grade and our team delivers an amazing product day in and day out. Smoking meat is all about intuition, because temperatures will never give you the same results. You will probably pull the pork butt out too early a few times before you pull out the perfect one."

Chef Chris says, "The restaurant is the first in the area to employ a new American barbecue mindset which means blending influences of an American melting pot into the old standards. To many, barbecue is a religion. We consider ourselves to be, non-denominational!"

Method —

Smoker Preparation: Rub pork butt thoroughly with seasoning, using it all. Preset your smoker preset at 225°F to cook. Place pork butt on smoker grate and continue feeding the fire. rotating for about 16 hours. Pork temperature should read 185°F. Once it starts to rise past this temperature it is done. Be sure to let the meat rest up to two hours. Once pork butt has rested, shred the meat and discard the bone if you have one. Drizzle your favorite BBQ sauce over the meat, mixing well.

Plating: Pile the pulled pork on a toasted Pretzel Brioche or your favorite toasted bun. Add your favorite slaw, sliced red onion (optional), pickle and more of your favorite BBQ sauce.

Wine and Spirit Pairing —

A shot of your favorite bourbon or a de Bine Hefeweizen on draft

Chef Chris Artrip   Zachery Feinstein

The Living Room

Dunedin on Main

Bouillabaisse

SERVES 4

Broth:
2 cans San Marzano whole tomatoes (28-ounces each)
2 oranges sliced
2 onions sliced
3 bulbs fennel julienne, reserve fonds
1 bottle Chardonnay
2 quarts water
1 pinch saffron
2 tablespoons extra virgin olive oil
3 dried Calabrian chili peppers (optional)
2 pounds lobster bodies
  or 2 tablespoons lobster base

Seafood:
4 lobster tails
12 medium-to-large shrimp
1½ pounds PEI Mussels
1 pound little neck clams
12 ounces fish Cobia

Garlic Butter:
2 pounds butter
4 garlic cloves
1 bunch parsley
1 baguette

The Living Room is located in the heart of Dunedin on Main Street, and features an eclectic menu of dishes inspired by cuisine from around the world, as well as an upscale yet relaxing dining room atmosphere. Open for lunch, dinner and brunch on the weekends, Chef Jordan Rivera says, "We invite you to come unwind, indulge and enjoy your very own culinary journey, guided by your expert server. Let us host or cater your next event. You will enjoy dining on our large patio where you can bring your dogs, as we even have a menu for your furry friends."

Method —

Broth: Heat Oven to 400°F. Toss oranges, onions and fennel in a large mixing bowl with a few generous splashes of extra virgin olive oil. Transfer to a sheet tray. Lay fresh thyme over oranges, fennel and onions, lightly seasoning with kosher salt. Roast for 12 to 15 minutes. After fennel, oranges and onions are in the oven, combine the rest of the broth ingredients in a large stock pot and cook on medium heat. Transfer fennel, oranges and onions to stock pot. Reduce on low for 45 minutes. Strain and return to the pot.

Garlic Butter: Add garlic and butter in food processor until smooth. Transfer to a container. Cut baguette on a bias into two-inch slices. Place on a sheet tray and lightly brush garlic butter on baguette slices and toast in 400°F oven for 6 to 8 minutes.

Seafood: To a large colander add mussels and clams, running cold water over the mix while removing the beards from the mussels and any graininess from the clams. Split lobster tails and run under cold water. Pat lobster tails dry, placing them on sheet tray to roast. Brush with butter garlic mixture and cook in 400°F oven for 6-8 minutes. While lobsters are in the oven cooking get shrimp and Cobia ready. Devein shrimp, leaving tails on and slice the Cobia thin into 1½-inch pieces. Return stock pot to medium heat. Once stock is simmering add Cobia. Wait 2 minutes, then add mussels and clams. Wait 2 minutes, then add shrimp. Cover for 3 to 4 minutes, taking shrimp out if you need to avoid overcooking.

Plating: Divide clams, mussels, Cobia, shrimp and lobster tails into four bowls, covering and pouring broth. Garnish with crostinis, lemon and fennel fonds.

Wine and Spirit Pairing —
Archery Summit Chardonnay

Chef Jordan Rivera   Zachery Feinstein

Marguerite's Café & Catering

Dunedin

Cilantro Lime Grilled Chicken

SERVES 6

6 boneless chicken breast halves

Marinade
¼ cup olive oil
¼ cup key lime juice
2 tablespoons chopped cilantro
1 tablespoons brown sugar
1 chopped scallions or red onion
½ teaspoon chopped lime zest
½ teaspoon ground pepper
Salt to taste

Salad
5 cups mixed greens of your choice
½ cup sliced strawberries
½ seeded cucumber sliced
1 grape tomato cut in half
¼ red onion sliced thin
¼ cup toasted sliced almonds

Mango Balsamic Dressing
¾ cup olive oil
¼ cup balsamic vinegar
⅛ cup Monin mango syrup
½ teaspoon garlic power
¼ teaspoon onion power
Pinch of red pepper and salt

Marguerite's started small and grew slowly to include the Café as well as their catering business, which was established 26 years ago. They offer take out, patio dining and a range of upscale to down home comfy food. Let Marguerite's cater, create, plan and make your next event perfect, drawing from their diverse menu, with recipes for all occasions.

Owner Marguerite Allison says, "Growing up in Michigan and traveling around the area as a young girl, I try to bring those Midwestern values and my Italian heritage to some of my dishes. We use fresh and seasonal ingredients, and each week offer a different choice from our delicious Specials Menu."

Marguerite's features the best of The Sunshine State's seasonal fresh fruit such as mangos, strawberries, kumquats, and Florida avocados. Their Signature Recipe is Cilantro Lime Grilled Chicken, the chicken carefuly marinated in fresh cilantro and lime. Marguerite's also uses fresh strawberries with mango dressing in their salad.

Method —

Marinade: In a bowl, combine and whisk all ingredients. Taste and adjust seasoning to taste.

Chicken: Place chicken breast between two sheets of plastic wrap and pound 'til flattened. Arrange the chicken in a shallow baking dish and pour marinade over, turning so as to coat the chicken completely. Cover and refrigerate for two hours.

Prepare grill for medium to high heat. Remove chicken from marinade and place on the grill for 7 to 10 minutes, turning once. Alternatively, chicken may be broiled in the oven.

Salad Dressing: Combine all ingredients in a blender.

Plating: Can be served with additional recipe of marinade which is thickened with one tablespoon of cornstarch and drizzled over chicken. Also good served with your favorite mango salsa.

Wine and Spirit Pairing —

Pinot Grigio

Marguerite Allison

Chef Wm. G. Forte

Marker 8 "On the Water" Tiki Bar & Grill

THE BEST WATERFRONT TIKI BAR IN DUNEDIN is located on Saint Joseph Sound at the Beso Del Sol Resort. Kick back and enjoy a bite to eat or a drink at Dunedin's famous Tiki Bar & Grill on Florida's Gulf Coast.

Marker 8 Tiki Bar and Grill serves up casual fare, cold beer, specialty drinks and fun seven days a week. From their awesome Cuban sandwich to their huge half-pound cheeseburger, you won't go hungry at Marker 8.

Bartenders mix the best Rumrunners from Tampa to Key West, plus they feature live music on the weekends, weather permitting.

Toast another golden day with your new friends at Marker 8 with a free sunset shot daily! Arrive by car, Jolly Trolley or by boat. Free docking for Marker 8 patrons. We are Dunedin's only dockside carryout food and liquor delivery service.

Spirits and Casual Fare Pairing Guide

TEQUILA MADE ME DO IT	Marker 8 Margarita	Kickin' Jalapeno	Strawberry Rita	Ruby Margarita	Skinny Minny	Cucumber Lime Margarita
DRAFT BEER	Rotating Beer	Goose Island	Shack Top	Landshark	Reef Donkey	Bud Select
BEERS AND MORE	Budweiser	Jai Lai	White Claw	Ciders	Heineken	Guinness
WINES	Chardonnay	Cabernet Sauvignon	Sauvignon Blanc	Sangria	Pinot Grigio	House Blend
FROZEN DRINKS	Piña Colada	Daiquiri	Life's A Mango	Bushwacker	Key Lime Colada	Raspberry Peach Strawberry
I THINK I'LL HAVE IT	Our Rum Runner	Dunedin Sunset	Sunshine Mule	Sundrop	Tiki Strawberry Lemonade	Malibu Bucket
FOOD	Cuban Sandwich	Burgers	Chicken Wings	Variety of Wraps	Catch of The Day	Tacos
	Peel & Eat Shrimp	Quesadillas	Seasonal Salads	Clam Strips	Sweet Potato Fries & Waffle Fries	Shrimp Cocktail

Mykonos

Authentic Greek Cookery

Lamb Youvetsi

SERVES 2

2 large lamb shanks
2 sweet onions diced
3 large tomatoes diced
½ bunch parsley chopped
1 cinnamon stick
2 bay leafs
¼ ounce oregano
4 tablespoons olive oil
½ cup red wine
1½ cups of water
1 pound of Misko Orzo
   (rice shaped pasta)
Salt and pepper to taste

Mayerion Mykonos' Cookery is the most authentic Greek restaurant in Tarpon Springs, Florida, which is known for its Greek heritage and as the Sponge Capital of the World.

In 1992, Andreas and Renee Salivaras moved to Tarpon Springs to open a restaurant and chose this community because it reminded them of their home. They immigrated from the Greek Island of Kimolos which is located in the Aegean Sea and part of the Greek southwest islands, specifically the island group known as the Cyclades, near the bigger island called Milos.

The Salivaras Family prides itself on creating Greek dishes, all made in house using the freshest ingredients. Andreas says, "Mykonos is their home and each one of our guests are family. The restaurant was built with love and is known by locals as, 'The place to eat.' Our Lamb Youvetsi takes time so you must be patient with the preparation."

Customers report that great hospitality is what they like most about dining at Mykonos.

"We look forward to seeing you all soon at Mykonos — Kali Orexi!"

Method —

Pre-heat oven to 400°F. Place lamb shanks in oven to brown. This is done to sweat out blood so that the meat does not have a gamey taste. In a large saucepan heat olive oil and add small diced onions and chopped parsley. Cook until onions have clarified. Add diced tomatoes, cinnamon stick, bay leaf, red wine and oregano. Cook down for 40 minutes on low to medium heat. Place shanks in an oven pan and pour sauce over the shanks. Cover and bake at 325°F for 90 minutes.

Once the lamb shanks have finished cooking, take shanks out of sauce and set aside. Add orzo to the sauce, then add water and stir. Bake covered at 325°F for 30 minutes, then add shanks back into the sauce with pasta. Bake for an additional 10 minutes and enjoy!

Wine and Spirit Pairing —

Domaine Costa Lazaridi, Amethystos

Andreas Salivaras

The Ozona Pig

Palm Harbor

Boss Hog Special

SERVES 2-4

4 Hickory smoked pork spare ribs
Half hickory smoked chicken
½ pound pulled pork
½ pound beef brisket
8 ounces BBQ baked beans
8 ounces coleslaw
2 deviled eggs

BBQ Sauces:
"Original"
"Some Like It Hot"
"Sweetie" Southern Style

Deviled Eggs:
Hard boiled eggs
Mayonnaise
Brown spicy mustard
Hint of Tabasco
Paprika for garnish

Located in the heart of historic Ozona — one of the oldest communities in Pinellas County — Chris and Bobbie Painter opened The Ozona Pig in 2004. A family tradition, their Southern Style Bar-B-Que is influenced by Memphis roots and the original Bobby's Bar-B-Que located in Fort Myers, Florida.

They show their love for cooking and sharing through their legacy BBQ, mouthwatering grilled rib eye, fresh garden salads, homemade banana pudding, and many other family favorites.

Family favorites come together with *The Boss Hog Special* named after the founder, Chris Painter, *aka Boss Hog*. Slow-cooked Hickory Smoked Spare Ribs, Chicken, Pulled Pork and Beef Brisket are complimented by homemade BBQ Baked Beans, Coleslaw and two Deviled Eggs.

Method —

The pork butt and beef brisket are gently dusted with "Sweetie Rub" and cooked in a Southern Pride Smoker at 250°F for 14 hours, with light smoke of Hickory and Black Jack Oak. The ribs and chicken get the same loving treatment, cooked at 250°F for four to six hours. Ozona Pig's legacy BBQ Baked Beans, Coleslaw and "Original BBQ Sauce" come from Bobby Bullard, Bobby's Bar-B-Que, Fort Myers, Florida. Best for last, are grandmother's Deviled Eggs.

Thanks Chris and Dad for this Family Legacy. The Ozona Pig is everything we love — good friends, good food and good conversation. Bring your family, bring your friends and we'll... meet ya' at the Pig."

Wine and Spirit Pairing —

Local Craft Brew, LaCrema Pinot Noir and Sweet Tea

Bobbie Painter, Proprietress

Palm Café

Dunedin Fine Art Center

New England Lobster Roll

SERVES 1

1 pound fresh lobster
1 stalk celery
1 tablespoon mayonnaise
1 teaspoon lemon juice
Salt and Pepper to taste
Iceberg lettuce shredded
Soft roll

Located in the atrium lobby of the Dunedin Fine Art Center, the Palm Café has made a name for itself as the perfect spot for breakfast and lunch. This hidden gem is operated by Chef Brian and Heather Healey, a talented team that has years of experience and a menu that would make even the most demanding foodie smile.

The menu offers freshly made entrées from top quality ingredients at prices that even a starving artist can afford. There is a wide variety of menu options from which to choose: homemade soups, salads, sandwiches, and there are always daily specials. They offer fruit smoothies, or vegan and gluten-free protein drinks — a perfect complement to your meal.

You can dine inside or out on the patio. Whichever you choose, the Palm Café will become one of your favorite places to eat.

Meet a friend at the Palm Café for breakfast, lunch or any special occasion. Then enjoy walking through the Dunedin Fine Art Center viewing the latest artists' exhibits.

Chef Brian's signature dish is a perfectly prepared Lobster Roll served on his freshly baked bread.

Method —

Fill a pan with water that covers the lobster adding a dash of salt. Bring the water to a rolling boil and cook for about 8 minutes. Do not cover. Remove and let the lobster rest for 5 minutes or so after cooking to allow the meat to absorb some of the moisture from the shell.

Shell lobster meat and dice into large pieces. (Do not use frozen lobster!)

In a mixing bowl add lobster, chopped celery, mayonnaise and lemon juice, then salt and pepper to taste. Toast a butter roll, then add lobster meat with some shredded lettuce on top.

Wine and Spirit Pairing —

Beer of your choice

Heather Healey

Chef Brian Healey

Pan y Vino

Brick Oven Pizza

Posse's Pesto Pie

SERVES 2

One pizza dough (10-inch pie)
1 cup Pesto sauce
1 cup sautéed Portobello mushrooms
1 diced shallot
10 basil leaves
½ cup crumbled Goat cheese
½ cup Mozzarella cheese
16 baby spinach leaves
½ cup diced small tomatoes

Pesto Sauce:
2 cups basil
½ head of garlic
1 pinch of salt
½ cup high-quality Pecorino Romano cheese
½–1 cup extra virgin olive oil

Pan y Vino Brick Oven Pizza Restaurant and Wine Bar on Main Street in Dunedin, Florida was the original location for Casa Tina's Mexican Restaurant, which began serving customers in 1992. Owners Javier and Tina Avila renovated the building in 2009, and today they serve delicious personal pizzas and wine by the glass. Tina says, "Our children grew up in our booths, and peeled tomatoes for chore money. This original restaurant space will forever remain in our hearts."

"These recipes are our own original creations from home. It is our love of cooking and passion for wine that inspired us to create Pan y Vino. Always important are fresh and unique ingredients — the smell of fresh basil, the feel of the elasticity of our pizza dough and the aroma of sautéed wild mushrooms fills the air and feeds your spirit."

Posse's Pesto Pie is one of Pan y Vino's customer favorites. The combination of wild mushrooms, goat cheese and aromatic pesto make for a mouthwatering and unforgettable pizza. The lushness of goat cheese is perfectly paired with a sharp sauvignon blanc or a bright pinot grigio.

With their white linen tablecloths and charming atmosphere, Pan y Vino's quaint space is the perfect setting for dining with family or friends, or a romantic night out.

Method —

Sauce: Combine all sauce ingredients in a food processor until liquefied.

Spread pesto sauce evenly to cover pizza dough. Evenly distribute slightly sautéed Portobello mushrooms with cooked shallots over pizza dough. Layer a few fresh basil leaves on pizza then sprinkle crumbled Goat cheese, Mozzarella cheese, diced tomatoes and baby spinach leaves on top.

Cook in a pizza oven or under broiler for desired darkness of crust.

Wine and Spirit Pairing —

Benvolio Pinot Grigio

Tina Marie Avila   Chef Javier Avila

Sea Sea Riders Restaurant

Dunedin on Main

Crusted Pecan Grouper

SERVES 1

Filet
7 ounces Grouper filet
3 ounces crushed pecans
¼ cup Panko breadcrumbs
Honey and mustard
Salt and pepper to taste

Mashed Potatoes
2 sweet potatoes
Dash cinnamon
Dash nutmeg
1 tablespoon dark brown sugar
2 tablespoons butter

Bourbon Sauce
3 ounces bourbon
3 tablespoons butter

Garnish
Candied pecans

How fitting that Sea Sea Riders has stood the test of time with outstanding service and great support from the community. Family owned and operated since 1988, Sea Sea Riders has served award-winning, reasonably-priced cuisine since the tumble weeds were blowing down Main Street in Dunedin, Florida.

Owners Sylvia and Artie Tzekas say, "We get better every year and have always prided ourselves on staying true to our old coastal Florida, done right, scratch kitchen. It is all about the food, the environment and the people."

"Our signature dish is Crusted Pecan Grouper which is a locally inspired dish. Enjoy the freshly caught grouper with a chardonnay or one of the vast selections of IPA beers or whiskeys at the large open bar or on our outdoor patio. You can also enjoy our award-winning, *'Best Cocktail In America'* Blueberry Yum Yum as voted by *Restaurant Hospitality Magazine*."

Method —

Filet: Mix crushed pecans and breadcrumbs together is a small bowl to make a pecan crust. Rinse off fish and dry well a with paper towel then season filet with salt and pepper. Mix some honey and mustard to taste and coat the filet on all sides. Roll filet in the crushed pecans and breadcrumbs mixture (pecan crust), pressing filet lightly to cover completely.

Preheat your oven to 350°F. Brown the crusted filet in a buttered saucepan, cooking both sides until brown. Finish filet in the oven for about 5 to 7 minutes or until flaky.

Sweet Potatoes Mash: Peel the sweet potatoes and boil. Mash potatoes and add cinnamon, nutmeg, butter and brown sugar.

Brown Butter Bourbon Sauce: In a saucepan melt the butter and bourbon, cooking the sauce until it foams.

Plating: Place the fish on top of the sweet potato mash, drizzling the brown butter bourbon sauce over the filet. Add candied pecans as garnish.

Spirit Pairing —

Pairs well with a Bleach Blonde Ale and Hemingway's Whiskey.

Sylvia Tzekas

Sonder Social Club

Dunedin

Braised Beef Short Ribs

SERVES 10-12

Braised Beef Short Ribs:
4 pounds bone in short ribs
¼ pound fresh ginger (sliced into rounds)
6 each star anise
2 tablespoons Sesame oil (for frying)
4 tablespoons Canola oil (for frying)
10-12 Steamed Buns (find at Asian Market)
10-12 teaspoon Lao Ga Ma Chili Crisp
    (Walmart or Amazon)

Short Rib Rub:
½ cup kosher salt
2 tablespoons coarse ground black pepper

Short Rib Liquid for Braising:
3 Tamarind Soda bottles (12.5 ounces each)
Water to cover the ribs
¼ pound fresh ginger (slice in the round)
1 tablespoon Szechuan peppercorns

Daikon Ginger Slaw:
1 carrot large
¼ bunch chopped cilantro
2 seeded jalapenos (cut in half)
1 Daikon radish large
1 red pepper (seeded and julienned)
4 inches grated ginger
2 ounces white sugar
4 ounces rice wine vinegar
1 julienned red onion

Sonder Social Club is the first craft cocktail bar in North Pinellas County and their food items are not typical of the normal "County Fare." The cuisine is decidedly mid-century modern minus the aspic and Jell-O salads. The dishes aren't just good; they are thoughtful and calculated — made to complement their unique drink program.

The Club's bar area is always humming — people loving the atmosphere. Though busy, there is still plenty of room to socialize at the bar, or you can enjoy the outside seating area. The bookcase shelves are lined with weathered volumes of The Classics, colorful vases and other unusual knick knacks. Give one of these shelves a nudge and you'll be on your way to the "loo'!"

Sonder Social Club is also Dunedin's newest craft cocktail lounge, opened August 2019, and one of the latest super high-quality ventures for The Feinstein Group.

"The Braised Beef Short Ribs are one of my favorite dishes," says Chef Christopher Artrip, "and basically anything you put Chili Crisp on is going to be delicious."

Method —

Cooking Ribs: Rub the short ribs with the rub ingredients. Preheat two large sauté pans using Sesame and Canola oil. Once the pan is simmering hot, put the ribs in and sear on all sides until dark brown, but not burnt. Transfer to a pan that will enable a complete covering with the braising liquid. Heat oven to 325°F and cook for 4 hours. While the ribs are cooling take the braising liquid and strain it into a stockpot and reduce. Cook the liquid on high heat. Reduce till there is maybe ⅛ of the original volume. Do not let the liquid caramelize at the bottom. Once the fat is skimmed off, shred the meat and mix into the liquid.

Slaw: Slice the Daikon radish twice as thick as the carrot. Suggest you use a mandolin. Mix all ingredients in a mixing bowl and let stand for 5-10 minutes in the refrigerator before serving.

Plating: Steam bun until softened. Add the short ribs. Top with Lao Ga Ma Chili Crisp then add the slaw.

Wine and Spirit Pairing —

N.T.S. (Reyka Vodka, Lemongrass, Mint, White Grapes and Champagne)

Chef Chris Artrip   Zachery Feinstein

The chefs featured in *Savor A Taste of Florida's West Coast* have offered a wine or spirit pairing to accompany their dish.

STIRLING WINE started in 2005 and has evolved from a themed gift shop selling Florida fruit wines, to what is now the Premiere Wine Bar in Downtown Dunedin, featuring boutique wines from around the world. Owners Rob and Luanne Haver say, "We are the locals' favorite, with a growing Wine Club where members are able to savor wines from renowned regions of France, Italy, Spain and North and South America. Our guests enjoy an expanding menu of artisan meats and cheeses, including a selection of imported and domestic beers." Visit Stirling Wine and enjoy the intimate outdoor patio supporting the best local musicians in the Tampa Bay area.

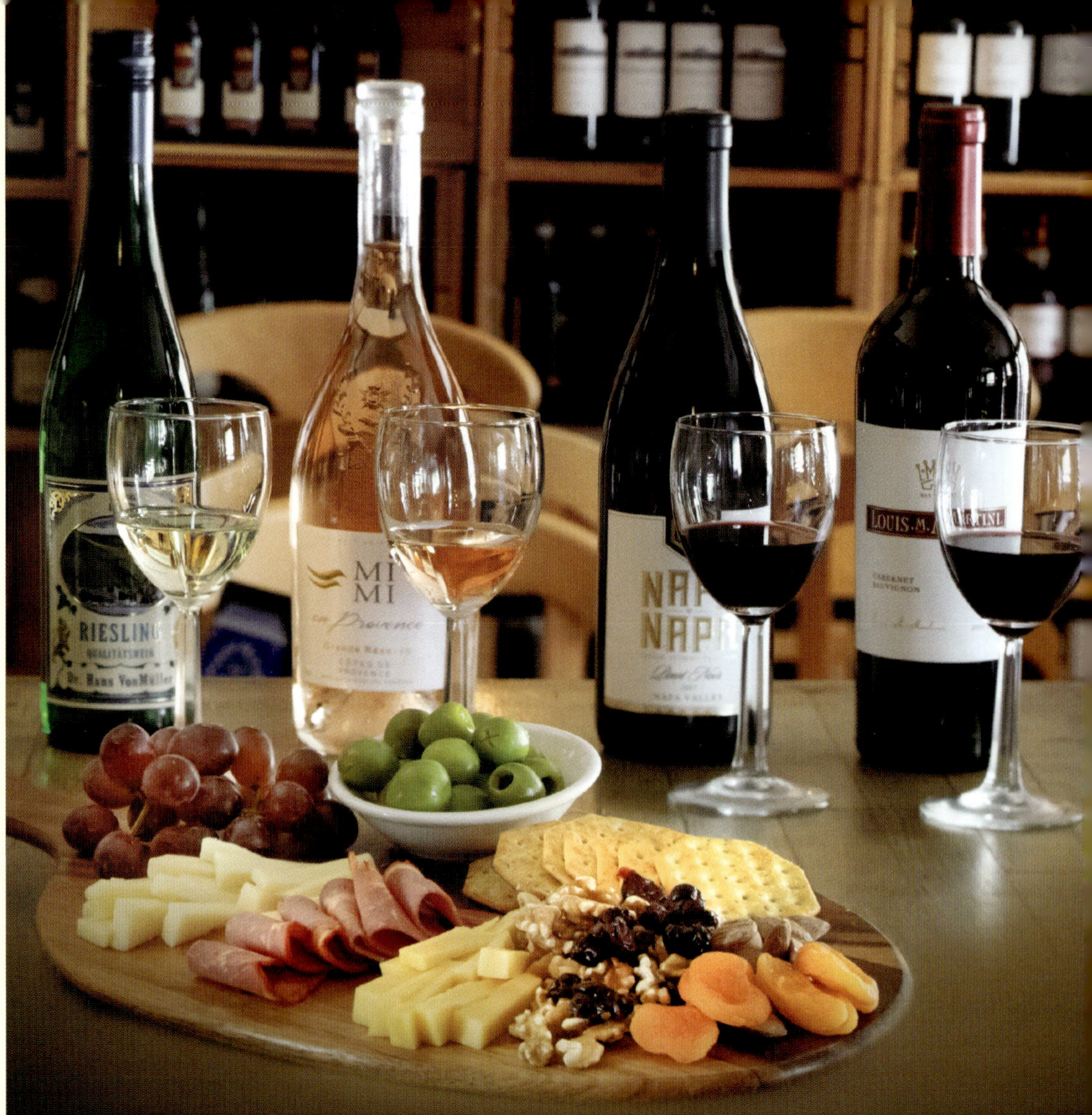

Stirling Wine
Featured Wine Bar in Downtown Dunedin

Wine and Food Pairing Guide

	SAUVIGNON BLANC	CHARDONNAY	RIESLING	PINOT NOIR	PINOT GRIGIO	MERLOT	CABERNET SAUVIGNON	ZINFANDEL
CHEESES & NUTS	Feta, Goat Cheese, Pine Nuts	Asiago, Havarti, Almonds	Havarti, Gouda, Candied Walnuts	Goat Cheese, Brie, Walnuts	Gruyère, Buffalo Mozzarella, Almonds	Parmesan, Romano, Chestnuts	Cheddar, Gorgonzola, Walnuts	Brie, Aged Cheese
MEAT OR FOWL	Chicken, Turkey	Veal, Chicken, Pork	Smoked Sausage, Duck	Lamb, Sausage, Filet Mignon, Chicken	Chicken, Turkey	Grilled Meats, Steak	Venison, Rib Eye, Beef Stew	Pork, Spicy Sausage, Beef, Duck
SEAFOOD	Sole, Oysters, Scallops	Halibut, Shrimp, Crab	Sea Bass, Trout	Orange Roughy, Tuna	Salmon, Scallops, Sea Bass	Grilled Swordfish, Tuna	Grilled Tuna	Cioppino, Blackened Fish
VEGETABLES & FRUIT	Citrus, Green Apple, Asparagus	Potato, Apple, Squash, Mango	Apricots, Chili Peppers, Pears	Mushrooms, Dried Fruit, Figs, Strawberries	Asparagus, Fennel, Capers, Pineapple	Caramelized Onions, Tomatoes, Plums	Black Cherries, Broccoli, Tomatoes	Cranberries, Grilled Peppers, Eggplant
HERB & SPICES	Chives, Tarragon, Cilantro	Tarragon, Sesame, Basil	Rosemary, Ginger	Nutmeg, Cinnamon, Clove	Basil, Cilantro, Parsley	Mint, Rosemary, Juniper	Rosemary, Juniper, Lavender	Pepper, Nutmeg
SAUCES	Citrus, Light Sauces	Cream Sauce, Pesto	Sweet BBQ, Spicy Chutney	Mushroom Sauce, Light-Medium Red Sauce	Light Sauces, Carbonara	Bolognese, Béarnaise	Brown Sauce, Tomato Sauce	Spicy Cajun, Salsa
DESSERTS	Sorbet, Key Lime Pie	Banana Bread, Vanilla Pudding	Apple Pie, Caramel Sauce	Crème Brûlée, White Chocolate	Poached Pears, Coconut Cake	Dark Chocolate, Berries, Fondue	Bittersweet Chocolate, Espresso Gelato	Spice Cake, Gingerbread, Carrot Cake

7venth Sun Brewery
1012 Broadway
Dunedin, FL 34698
727.733.3013
7VENTHSUN.COM

Bayou Bistro & Tiki Bar *ON WATER & BOAT ACCESS
607 Island Drive
Tarpon Springs, FL 34689
727.940.6120
BAYOUBISTROANDTIKI.COM

The Black Pearl
315 Main Street
Dunedin, FL 34698
727.734.3463
THEBLACKPEARLDUNEDIN.COM

Bon Appétit *ON WATER
148 Marina Plaza
Dunedin, FL 34698
727.733.2151
BONAPPETITRESTAURANT.COM

Café Alfresco *ON TRAIL
344 Main Street
Dunedin, FL 34698
727.736.4299
CAFEALFRESCO.COM

Caledonia Brewing
587 Main Street
Dunedin, FL 34698
727.351.5105
CALEDONIABREWING.COM

Carmelita's Mexican Grill & Cantina
1280 Main Street
Dunedin, FL 34698
727.240.4946
CARMELITASMEXICANGRILL.COM

Casa Tina
365 Main Street
Dunedin, FL 34698
727.734.9226
CASATINAS.COM

Cotherman Distilling Company *ON TRAIL
933 Huntley Avenue
Dunedin, FL 34698
727.523.0555
COTHERMANDISTILLING.COM

Cueni Brewing Company *ON TRAIL
945 Huntley Avenue
Dunedin, FL 34698
727.266.4102
CUENIBREWING.COM

Currents Restaurant *ON TRAIL
200 E. Tarpon Avenue
Tarpon Springs, FL 34689
727.940.5377
CURRENTS-TARPON.COM

Dimitri's On the Water *ON THE WATER
690 Dodecanese Boulevard
Tarpon Springs, FL 34689
727.945.9400
FACEBOOK.COM

Dunedin Brewery
937 Douglas Avenue
Dunedin, FL 34698
727.736.0606
DUNEDINBREWERY.COM

Dunedin Coffee Company & Bakery
730 Broadway, Suite #3
Dunedin, FL 34698
727.286.6147
DUNEDINCOFFEECO.COM

Dunedin Golf Club Fairway Grille & 19th Hole
1050 Palm Boulevard
Dunedin, FL 34698
727.733.2134
DUNEDINGOLFCLUB.COM

Flanagan's Irish Pub
465 Main Street
Dunedin, FL 34698
727.401.3477
FLANAGANSIRISHPUB.NET

HEW Parlor & Chophouse at Fenway Hotel
453 Edgewater Drive
Dunedin, FL 34698
727.683.5990
FENWAYHOTEL.COM

HOB Brewing Company *ON TRAIL
931 Huntley Avenue
Dunedin, FL 34698
727.216.6318
HOB.BEER.COM

H'ours Creole Smokehouse
310 E. Tarpon Avenue
Tarpon Springs, FL 34689
727.483.9092
HOURSCREOLE.COM

Iron Oak New American BBQ
917 11th Street
Palm Harbor, FL 34683
727.754.7337
IRONOAKBBQ.COM

The Living Room
487 Main Street
Dunedin, FL 34698
727.736.5202
THELIVINGROOMONMAIN.COM

Marguerite's Café & Catering
405 Plaza Drive
Dunedin, FL 34698
727.734.7040
MARGUERITESCATERING.COM

Marker 8 On the Water Tiki Bar & Grill *ON WATER & BOAT ACCESS
1420 Bayshore Boulevard
Dunedin, FL 34698
727.738.5000
MARKER8.COM

Mykonos
628 Dodecanese Boulevard
Tarpon Springs, FL 34689
727.934.4306
FACEBOOK.COM

The Ozona Pig
311 Orange Street
Palm Harbor, FL 34683
727.773.0744
OZONAPIG.COM

Palm Café at Dunedin Fine Art Center
1143 Michigan Boulevard
Dunedin, FL 34698
727.298.3322
DFAC.ORG

Pan y Vino Brick Oven Pizza
369 Main Street
Dunedin, FL 34698
727.734.7700
FACEBOOK.COM/PANYVINODUNEDIN

Sea Sea Riders
221 Main Street
Dunedin, FL 34698
727.734.1445
SEASEARIDERSDUNEDIN.COM

Soggy Bottom Brewing Company
662 Main Street
Dunedin, FL 34698
727.601.1698
SOGGYBOTTOMBREWING.COM

Sonder Social Club
966 Douglas Ave, Unit #101
Dunedin, FL 34698
727.754.6674
SONDERSOCIAL.CLUB

Stirling Wine
461 Main Street
Dunedin, FL 34698
727.734.4025
STIRLINGWINEDUNEDIN.COM

Woodwright Brewing Company
985 Douglas Avenue
Dunedin, FL 34698
727.238.8717
WOODWRIGHTBREWING.COM

A THANK YOU NOTE

A book like this doesn't happen overnight. It has been a careful process with many months of design and creative development. There are so many people I would like to acknowledge for their inspiration, enthusiasm, support, commitment and friendship.

I thank my longtime friend and gifted graphic designer, Thomas Granade, for his spirit, generosity and vision which has helped to make this book truly elegant.

My world class photographer, Stephen Kovich, infused his unique photography expertise to make this book such an exquisite collection of food presentations. Stephen somehow found the time to go the extra mile, and make sure that all of the participants were happy with the imagery created for them.

I would like to thank finally, all of the brewers, chefs, owners and restaurateurs who contributed their signature dishes for all of us to enjoy, and for sharing their stories of "How" they are fulfilling their dreams, and for opening their doors to me, thus supporting my dream to highlight some of the best recipes and dining experiences in Dunedin, Palm Harbor and Tarpon Springs, and the world!

The idea for *Savor a Taste of Florida's West Coast, Signature Restaurant Recipes,* started with the 50th Anniversary celebration of the Dunedin History Museum, and my decision to help by donating books to sell in their Station Shop. Who knew that this simple inspiration could produce such a fun and memorable book.